Brighten a

Senior's Day I

D1125227

ANGELIKA SCHWARZ

Cover- Graphic Design, illustrations and photos
by Angelika Schwarz

ISBN-10: 1518788122

ISBN-13: 978-1518788123

This little book is from me to **me**,
Or from me to **you**.

Don't matter if me or who.
Most is made-up …
and some is true.

I wrote the poems,
And the short stories too.

Stroll down memory lane,
And giggle at a few.

Hope you enjoy, and if you do;

Please
Let me know, in your Amazon review.
Angelika Schwarz

Brighten a Senior´s Day

DEDICATION

For My Mother

You left your laughter in my memories,

your wisdom in my deeds, and your

fingerprints of grace in my life.

CONTENTS

EYES ARE THE WINDOWS
TO OUR SOULS –

BUT IT'S OUR SMILES THAT ALLOW
US TO SHARE WHAT WE HOLD.

Spreading joy, understanding, and
compassion, even when we feel down,
can magically open the doors to our own
happiness.

It's not about the cards of life that have
been dealt to us, it's about how we deal the
cards to others.

ONE

TV ANTENNAS

Remember how antennas looked like
bunny ears.
They had hundreds of designs, alone at
Sears.

Flat bases, round ones, square, and many
more,
On the sets, they stood; as part of the
décor.

Now, just *ignore* television for a minute.
This is about design, and not what's in it.

On top of the TV was not only an antenna,
But a bowl with apples, pears and a banana.

Almost all had a photograph in a fancy
frame,
Of family, babies, or some sexy
dame.

Now TV's are getting more slender by the
year,
Contrary to my bum; it fills the chair with
ears.

Where shall we put all our plastic pink
roses?
We won at the fair, shooting red clown
noses?
The porcelain dancing figurine is lost by
the books,
Pirouetting between magazines – where
nobody looks.

Everyone is now watching a new digital
TV,
It's way too flat – even for a baby Kiwi!

Forget the plastic flowers and the Hummel
ornaments,
No more room for photos, antennas, and
candle stick scents.

From the digital boob tube, I turn my easy
chair away,
and smile at the shelves, where my
memories lay.

I close my eyes and ears to the flickering
screen,
And recall gone-by days - better than any
TV scene.

TWO

DANNY-BOY

(A TRUE STORY)

I looked at my eighteen-year old son and cupped his face in my hands. His eyes, just like his Dad's eyes, shimmered with held back tears. He got his fine straight nose from his grandfather; high cheekbones from his grandmother, and his wide smile, grinned back at my own wide smile.

"This is stupid," he said. "Ice hockey players don't cry."

"Did you pack Kleenexes?" I laughed a bit too forcefully.

Herbert, my husband, handed his son the last suitcase. Danny swung it on top of the other suitcases as if it were empty. His father clapped his hand on Danny's wide back.

I knew my husband was hurting. He had never missed a practice or game since Danny stood in the ice ring. Suddenly I had a flash of our son; three years old, clutching onto a chair, and pushing it along the ice to support himself. His over-sized ice hockey shirt fell down to his wobbly ankles, and his helmet looked like a bright beach ball set on top of his baby shoulders.

"I'll pretend you're sitting on those bleaches, watching me." Danny hugged his father. "What the heck will you do now with all your spare time?" He joked.

"I'll finally have time for your mother." Herbert turned and gave me a wink.

A honk resounded.

"Here they are." Danny said. He gave me one last hug. Our son climbed into the van, and mumbled, "I love you Mom, see you in a year or two."

My husband and I went to the van to say goodbye to the other players as well. Huge ice hockey bags lay between them. Over the past fifteen years we had all grown together like one big family. Ice hockey practice, games, camps, summer camps, Christmas and Halloween parties, organizing cake and hot dog stands were all things that had bonded us with the boys and their parents. At one of the summer camps, the boys nicknamed me Snow-White. We're your dwarfs, they had said, while hugging my legs, and munching on my home-baked chocolate chip cookies. Behind my smile, a deep wave of melancholy swept over me, as Danny and his friends waved good-bye, calling out my nickname, "Snow-White".

There we stood, Herbert and I, and watched the van drive away – honking madly, as if it were a happy occasion. We watched, till the van became a tiny dot in the horizon; and then we watched the empty street. We stood there arm in arm, trying to prolong the parting, in attempt to capture our son's aura, his cheerfulness, his light heartedness, his smell, his love his everything in our hearts in order to nurture us and comfort us in the emptiness of our home.

We turned and walked slowly back up the path to our house.

"I don't know how parents cope with their sons going to the military; or worse; going to war. Maybe Danny will be living on the other side of the world, but at least his life won't be in danger." I said, sensing I had to say something to comfort both of us.

My husband didn't say anything. He silently got a bottle of champagne from the refrigerator and poured two glasses. At that moment a song came on the radio, "Danny-boy." The song couldn't have come at a worse time.

My big burly husband crumbled down onto the kitchen chair and cried so hard that his shoulders shook. I took him in my arms and gently stroked his back. I have a new responsibility, I thought, while battling my own lump in my throat. I got to take care of my Hubby and make our life beautiful together.

We raised our glasses and saluted to a new beginning in our childless home.

***

It's two years later. Danny moved back home…but it was only a short stop, till he could find an apartment.

It was an adjustment having him back. The chaos in his room, the half-eaten pizzas lying around, non-stop telephone ringing, squeezed hair jell tubes and cologne bottles balancing dangerously along the bathroom sink. Soda drinks stood on every counter, and his awful techno music threatened our walls to crumble.

When the time came for him to leave again, we stood by our house and watched our son drive away to his new apartment. We watched him go; arm in arm, love in our hearts. But this time a deep sigh of relief accompanied that loving feeling.

 We grasped each other's hands as we walked up the path back to our house. Not till we went through the door, did we realize we were swinging our held hands back and forth like two playful children.

Suggestions for Discussions:

Do you remember leaving your parent's home for the first time? How old were you then?

Do you remember how you felt? Do you remember how your parents let you go?

Did you play any sports? What was your favorite sport?

Do you remember experiencing your own empty nest?

When did your last child leave your home?

Did you start a new hobby, or return to work when your children left your home?

THREE

LOVING NIGHTS

Do you remember those loving nights,

When just a touch would give you a shiver?

Flickering flames, soft candle lights,

The look of love in his eyes shimmered.

He would whisper tenderly in your ear;

And the words caused your heart to soar.

Your biggest wish was to have him near,

You never wanted him less – only more.

Now you see him in his comfy chair,

Reading his newspaper, spectacles on.

His tan is sallow – white and thin his hair.

You touch his arm – the feeling isn't gone.

Passion? No. It isn't the same.

We all wish that weren't really the case.

But when our man says that special nickname;

We slip into the silk gown adorned with lace.

We cuddle and sleep in each other's arms,

Knowing we love and it'll forever hold.

Not because of our looks or our charms

But for each other's care as we grow old.

With love in our hearts – gentle and kind,

We are needed and we need,

Purer than what young lovers could find,

Till the weaker one takes leave.

But that's the way nature is,

So be it…

We should be glad.

For if we had to choose

Who goes first..

That could make the other one sad.

FOUR

THE DIMPLED FIN

1970

"Joy to the World," the year's hit blasted for the umpteenth time out of the car radio. All windows and the car top were down in the rusty, blue, Dodge convertible. Bare feet, painted with hot pink nail polish, rested on the dashboard.

It was unusual that we both had a break, from flying at the same time. Mary and I were Pan Am stewardesses. We had a "complete" day off, which meant we didn't have to be glued to the phone, to be on call.

***

"Let's do something exciting!" I pulled the big flowered bed cover off her and onto the floor.

"Ride-on!" Mary said. She immediately sat up and ruffled her short blond hair. "Let's drive to the Gulf Coast!"

We slipped our mini beach dresses over our neon pink bikinis, slung our Mexican-canvas bags over our bare shoulders, and plopped wide-brimmed floppy hats onto our heads. The only touch of make-up that day was black eye-liner and pale pink; almost white lipstick, to accentuate our Florida tans.

We were roommates stationed near Miami Airport. Just the thought of taking a drive across the state of Florida was more thrilling than our usual shuttle flights to the Caribbean or South America. There we were; one 20 year old and a twenty-two year old stewardess, in the prime of our lives —living for the moment, and enjoying, what we thought would be a beautiful summer day in Florida.

Mary sped along the Alligator Highway. Seemed like we were the only people alive, no cars behind us; no cars coming towards us. We sang along with the radio; *"… joy to the fishes in the deep blue sea….."*

"Here," Mary handed me the cheap cold Bali wine. "Something to lubricate the vocal chords with."

I chugged a couple of mouthfuls, "Mmm better than honey."

The road seemed endless, but the time went fast. We were keenly aware of the warm wind in our non-sprayed hair, the happy hazy feeling from the wine. Just Mary and me, two best friends, and the world; we felt like we owned it.

"Do you know where you're going, Mary?" I asked.

"We'll stop, as soon as we get to a beach." Mary lay far back in the driver's seat and grabbed the steering wheel between her bare feet. In slow wide left and right swerves, she waltzed the car along the country highway.

"Do you know which beach?"

"No silly…but it's the Gulf Coast…it's all beach."

Mary was the boss between us two. She was two years older…and her voice was deeper than mine. I sat back into the plastic seat, and hung one leg out over the door. The sun was just beginning to set, as we rolled onto the sand straight ahead of us. We climbed out of the car, shed our dresses, sticky and crumpled from the ride, and ran into the cool water. I had to walk a long way in to get over my head. I turned to see if Mary was following me, but instead I saw her hopping up and down like a Jumping Jack on the beach.

I dove under to cool my head and surfaced, wondering why she wasn't in the water yet. Between thick wet strands of hair, I watched Mary run in a frenzied pattern, to the edge of the water and back again. She was screaming something. I was too far away and couldn't make out the words. Out of the blue, I watched two young men appear from between high bushes that grew along the coastline. I started to swim to shore. *Oh no*, I thought. *Those hippies are threatening her.* But then the guys started to yell as well and then I heard the word; "shark!"

Maybe it was the shock from my overheated body in the cool water, maybe it was the Bali wine and or the sun that beamed down on my head all day long, but I didn't panic. I looked around, and there it was; a shark fin, with a dent, like a dimple at the top, swimming about ten feet behind me. Without splashing, I breast swam to the beach; the shark maintaining the same distance between us. As soon as I could stand, I walked onto shore. The shark turned, the fin disappeared and left as quietly as he came.

"Oh my God", Mary cried. "Didn't you see what was following you?" She buckled onto her knees into the soft white sand.

The two strangers looked at me as if I were an apparition appearing before them. The setting sun transformed them and Mary into dark blue shadows. "Far out! A shark! What a trip, man," one of the hippies said. "Seeing you cumin' out of the water like that; so slow and cool. Freaked me out."

"Yeah, and the sun shining on you girl, all golden." said the other hippie. "Looked like one big halo around ya, man."

The only thing that entered my mind was one of the songs we repeatedly had been hearing on the radio along our drive. I began to sing softly: *"Put your hand in the hand of the man that stilled the waters"*... Mary got up and started to sing with me; *"Put your hand in the hand of the man who calmed the seas."* We all embraced; Mary, me, and the two hippies, that came from nowhere.

Close to tears, I untwined my arms from the others and turned towards the ocean. Between cupped hands, I called out in a choked voice: "Thank you dear, dumb, dimpled, shark for letting me live." I felt like the chosen one, and began a slow dance. The two hippies joined me, chanting something about the queen of sharks.

From the peaceful waters a splash resounded. Mary grabbed my arm. "Look, over there! Your shark is back!" She burst out laughing; "And ... he's smiling!" In the hazy evening light, the four of us watched a lonely dolphin emerge high up and out of the water; just long enough for us to see his friendly smile. He swam close to shore. Close enough for us to see the dimpled fin on his rounded gleaming back, before he glided back into the dark silky sea.

We sat on the beach a long time; hoping that our new friend would return. The magic of the night encompassed us as we spoke in hushed tones, under the million stars. We were in awe of nature and its spell-bounding mysteries. Our smiling friend didn't return that night, but he left behind a sprinkle of enchantment in our hearts, that has never faded.

Suggestions for Discussions:

Can you remember spending a long night under the stars?

Where was it? Who were you with?

What night sounds do you love?

FIVE

MASKS

The sensitivity of our souls is so very

fragile;

On the outside we may be cool and oh so

very casual.

But our outer visage is often a

mask

Disguising deep wounds, can be a

task.

What is essential to live with inner
peace?
I think I know. It's always within our
reach.

Rejoicing in just the little simple
things
Whether it's a sunbeam or how a child
sings.

It's the wind rustling leaves on a crisp fall
day,
An orange yellow sunset across a sandy
bay.

It's shaking off all burdens, for they too
will pass,

It's breathing in and out, just plain living at
last.
People will come and
disappear,
Touch your life and
then go.
In the end, it's only
you,

and
the mustard seeds
you've
sowed.

SIX

THE PUMPKIN GIRL

It was the first high school reunion that she had ever attended. Lisa entered the decorated gym. Many of the alumni glanced her way, but no one greeted her. At the refreshment stand, she poured herself a drink.

An obese bald guy approached her, and stared at her name tag. "Lisa Demon? Why don't I know you?"

"I know you", Lisa said, eyeing the man over her drink. "You were on the football team, right? Tod Baker."

"Were you a cheerleader?"

"Well, sort of. I was the girl who dressed up as a pumpkin for the Halloween football games."

"You got to be kidding me! What a waste of a beautiful girl."

"Well looks like the table has turned."

"What do you mean by that?"

"Now *you* look like a pumpkin, and you don't even need a costume. "

"That's not very nice." Tod scowled and stepped back.

"I know. You and your high school buddies weren't nice to me either." Lisa said, brushing her glossy black hair over her shoulder.

"So what are you going to do about it? Seek revenge?"

"Revenge? No, that's too simple."

Suddenly the lights dimmed. A cinema screen was pulled down from the ceiling. Lisa pushed her way through the crowd to the stage.

"Music please", she called. She grabbed a microphone and began to sing low and sexy, *"You are so beautiful to me..."* As she sung, the class photos of 1999 appeared in pale colors upon the screen. But the students weren't identifiable, for large pumpkins covered each face. The camera zoomed in, focusing on the names. Lastly, Lisa presented a snapshot of herself – fat, crying, and alone.

She stopped singing.

A drumroll filled the room, while on the screen, the pumpkin heads slowly rolled off the teenagers' shoulders, revealing how each student's face had aged in a most unsightly way.

Lisa looked around the room. "Most of you have teenagers at home," she said. "Tell your kids to treat their classmates with respect. Tell them they never really know who they're messing with – or what that person may become. And if your child should be a victim of mobbing, tell him or her about me; I'm Lisa – better known as the Pumpkin Girl."

Her eyes narrowed. "Your bullied child must never give up! Hard work and perseverance heals those wounds caused by oppression and intimidation!" The beautiful woman gesticulated toward the screen. "Your own pumpkin heads have just been removed! You're now free of the spells that I've been casting over you throughout the years!"

A high pitched laugh resounded from Lisa's ruby red lips. From the shadows, a tall man appeared and guided her out through the school's portals and into a dark stretch-limousine.

Through the glass doors, the dumbfounded class, of 1999, watched as the vehicle vanished, like a shooting star, into the yellow moon light.

Warily, the former classmates touched their own faces, while observing in astonishment one another's metamorphosis, as their faces slowly smoothed, their wide downward grimaces transformed to shy smiles, eye balls lost the yellow shimmer, and the frightening orange blotches faded, revealing a youthful new freshness. But most of all a gentle and genuine kindness filled their hearts, which spread in a magical aura around the class of 1999.

Suggestions for Discussions:

Did you go to costume balls??

What did you go as?

Can you remember a mask that you made

yourself or bought?

SEVEN

GRANDMA'S APRON JIG

Are you familiar with the poem Grandma's Apron? The original version was written by Tina Trivett, who wrote the poem in honor of her grandmother.

Tina Trivett's poem inspired me to write my *own* version… which I'll call…

Grandma's Apron Jig

Grandma's Apron Jig Recite or sing to the tune of Oh Susannah.	Oh, Susannah A minstrel song by Stephen Foster

I gaze at my new
kitchen,
Latest gadgets by
the score.
But nothing is so
handy,
As the smock, my
grandma wore.

*

Pure cotton white,
many pockets;
How deep –
nobody
knows.
Filled with
pencils, keys, and
lockets,
Rubber bands and

I come from
Alabama
With a banjo
on my knee
I'm going to
Louisiana,
My true love
for to see.

*

It rained all
night;
the day I left
The weather it
was dry
The sun so
hot, I froze to
death
Susannah,

pretty bows.

don't you cry.

*Oh my grandma,
you,
Taught me how to
be,
I cuddled in
you're lovin' arms,
You're forever
dear to me.*

*

Tiny hands
grabbing at the hem,
Guiding first
wobbly steps,
Spotted with yoke
and apple jam,
Sweet dreams in

*Oh, Susannah,
Oh don't you
cry for
me,
For I come
from Alabama
With a banjo
on my knee.*

*

I had a dream
the other night
When every-
thing was still
I dreamed I
saw Susannah
dear; A-coming

apron laps.

*

She hid her face
behind her skirt,
Play peekaboo
and giggle.
Rub tiny hands
free from dirt.
On her knees;
humpty-dumpty
jiggle.

*

*Oh my grandma,
you,
Taught me how to
be, I cuddled in
you're lovin' arms,
You're forever
dear to me.*

down the hill.

*

The buck-
wheat cake was
in her mouth;
The tear was in
her eye: Says
"I'm coming
from the south,
Susannah,
don't you cry."

*

*Oh, Susannah,
Oh don't you
cry for me
For I come
from Alabama
With a banjo*

*

Mixed with corn
husks and beans,
Baskets of flowers
from the hill,
Carried between
the sturdy seams,
Daisies upon the
sill.

*

She flapped her
apron at the kittens,
And used a corner
to wave good-bye.
She swapped the
flies to the dickens,
And dried a tear
from her eye.

*

on my knee.

*

I come from
Alabama
With a ban-jo
on my knee,
I'm going to
Louisiana, My
true love for to
see.

*

I come from
Alabama
With a banjo
on my knee
I'm going to
Louisiana,
My true love
for to see.

It could hold all
the play things,
Picked up from
the kitchen floor,
My oh my,
grandma would
sing;
"Apron so big,
room for more".

*

*Oh my grandma,
you,
Taught me how to
be,
I cuddled in
you're lovin' arms,
You're forever
dear to me.*

*

It rained all
night the day I
left
The weather it
was dry
The sun so
hot, I froze to
death
Susannah,
don't you cry.

*

*Oh, Susannah,
Oh don't you
cry for me
For I come
from Alabama
With a banjo*

*

She's scoop the

dust

from the table;

Wipe running

noses, sticky lips.

Brush those

crumbs, rub at

labels;

Needs no dish

cloth or baby bibs.

*

A warm cover on

chilly nights,

She chased away

all childish fears,

Catching kitten

from counter heights

Aprons grow

on my

knee.

*

I had a dream

the other night

When

everything was

still

I dreamed I

saw Susannah

dear

A-coming

down the hill.

*

The

buckwheat cake

was in her mouth

The tear was

in her eye

softer, through the years.

*

Oh my grandma, you,

Taught me how to be,

I cuddled in you're lovin' arms,

You're forever dear to me.

*

I gaze at my new kitchen,

Latest gadgets by the score.

But nothing is so handy,

Says I, "I'm coming from the south, Susannah, don't you cry."

*

Oh, Susannah,

Oh don't you cry for me

For I come from Alabama

With a banjo on my knee.

*

I come from Alabama

With a ban-jo on my knee,

I'm going to

as the smock, my
grandma wore.

*

*Oh my grandma,
you,
Taught me how to
be,
I cuddled in
you're lovin' arms,
You're forever
dear to me.*

Louisiana,
My true love
for to see.

*

*Oh, Susannah,
oh,
Don't you cry
for me,
For I come
from Alabama
With a banjo
on my knee.*

SEVEN

A NEON PINK REMOTE

"Hey Grandma! Catch this!" Deep hoarse laughter bellowed out of the car window.

"Oh man, does she ever need it!" They yelled after her.

I dropped my shopping bags, to catch a neon pink flying object.

"What is it?" I cried, stepping back as the car suddenly lifted in the air and hovered above me.

One of the teenagers leaned out of the window and cupped his hands around his mouth. "Press the *back* button to the year you would change in your life!"

"What the....! Who are you?" I shouted back.

"Human behaviour analyticians, Honey Pie!" They all croaked, and off they twirled, till they were just a speck in the clouds.

I looked around the Filene's parking lot. Empty! No witness in sight! The object felt heavy in the palm of my hand. It looked like remote control. In the middle of the display a *back* button glowed.

I stuffed the remote in my purse and quickly drove home. My three grandchildren were spending the day with me, and I was late all ready.

After clearing the picnic dishes and sending the children off to play in the garden, I snuggled into my porch swing. I couldn't believe I had the incredible opportunity to zap 43 years back to my college freshmen year! I knew now what I would study; film making, scriptwriting, and my biggest passion of all; illustrating and writing children's books.

But wait! I covered the remote with both hands.

Happy thoughts of me throwing my graduation cap in the air, were quickly pushed aside, as I pictured myself seeking a job in a world of hungry writers racing, neck to neck, to renowned agents and publishers. Fast forward. I see myself falling in love. Where will that be? Los Angeles? New York? Will the decision; career or children be a burden to me? I have struggled so hard to come so far. How could I ever give up this profession, this calling? How could I do both?

Fresh apple blossom scents spread in the warm spring breeze. I watched my three grandchildren. A sudden twinge shot through my heart. Their voices sounded hollow, their bright clothes began to fade. I realized they never would exist if I change my past.

My granddaughter skipped up the porch steps and gently took my hand. I quickly stuffed the remote between the potted red Geraniums. She led me to the picnic blanket where my two grandsons were patiently waiting.

"Tell us another story, Grandma, poleeeeease." With hopeful wide eyes, they cuddled onto my lap. Together, we entered a fantasy world of fairies and magic spells. I smiled down at their little trusting faces.

"Look Grandma!" Michael pointed toward our pond. On the edge of a rock sat a fat, grinning, bull frog. Between his front webbed feet, a pink remote gleamed in the sun.

"Rivet" it croaked. Or did he say; "Write it"? With a neon pink splash, he leaped into the pond, remote and all.

Good idea, I chuckled. I *should* write the fairy tales down that I've been telling my grandchildren over the years! I hugged my little audience, and asked them what they thought of their grandmother writing a children's book.

"Oh yes!" They clapped their hands excitedly.

And the moral of the story?

No dream is too **remote**.

And that ain't no ***bull****....frog.* ☺

Suggestions for Discussions:

If you had the chance to change your career, or your schooling – if you had such a magical remote; what would you have done? Would you change your past?

NINE

BEACH CHAIR

I breath in deeply the salty clean air,

The breeze gently lifts, and combs through
my hair.

My skin feels young, vibrant, and fresh.

I'm wearing my turquoise flowered summer
dress.

With bare toes I play with the foam from the
wave,
Snuggled in my beach chair on a warm sunny
day.

My book on my lap – can't get myself to read.
For the glistening ocean waves are all I want
to see.

MEN BACK THEN

Remember those cool ads of cowboys –
big and rugged.
Whiskey flasks by their sides,
ready to jug it.

Galloping off towards the sunsets;
in red and orange they would glow.
Through barren deserts, yellow prairies,
and mountains of sparkly snow.

They would hold their horses' reins lightly in
one gloved hand,
While hoofs thundered and manes flew, as
they crossed the lands.
And no matter where they were riding; east,
west, north or south,
A Camel cigarette hung out of the corner of
their mouth.

Smoke curled up, and made 'em shut one
crinkly eye,
Their teeth white and gleaming, ewwwweee;
My kind of guy!
Nothing could stop them, no heat or cold,
But me? I'm getting all flushed as this story is
told.

Suggestions for Discussions:

Did you have a favorite actor or actress who you were secretly in love with?

Did you enjoy western TV shows and movies?

What were your favorites?

Bonanza?

Long Ranger?

Roy Rogers?

Can you add any more names?

TEN

MARYBETH AND MR. PARKER

The old woman sat by her window and observed the leaves fluttering in the mild autumn wind. She watched while some seemed to cling on to the lower branches, and others just let go, sailing rapidly down, steering around any branch that may hold them back...

That's me, she thought, staring down at her gnarled veined hands. I'm just sailing down … down… No more branches for me. Yup, that's me.

The dinner gong resounded through the hall. She slowly stood up, remained a moment till her arthritic bones seemed to click in place and with small steps entered the hall to head for the dining area.

Today she will be seated at a new table. Feeling a little proud, that at least she remembered what the nurse's aide had told her. *Must be the new medication I'm taking*, she thought. She sighed, hoping that she won't have to talk much to the others. *Why bother —* she sighed again.

The nurse's aide placed her at an empty table with four chairs. "Isn't anyone else seated at this table?" Marybeth asked.

"Oh yes, he should be here any minute." The nurse bustled away, but not before she gave the little woman a knowing wink.

The soup was served, and the old woman blew carefully on her spoon, when through the steamy cloud, she observed a white haired man, slowly take his place across from her.

"Kathy?" he said with a wide smile, causing his blue eyes to crinkle into fine lines.

"No, I'm Marybeth." She said, smoothing the napkin on her lap. "Who are you?"

"Are you playing games with me again," he gave Marybeth a long happy look. He laid a rose by her soup bowl, took her hand from across the table, and gently kissed it.

"I'm sorry," Marybeth said, pulling her hand away. "You're mistaken, I'm Marybeth." She turned as a young nurse's aide sat on the empty chair by the old woman.

May I show you something?" The nurse's aide asked.

"What do you want to show me?" Marybeth looked puzzled.

The nurse's aide gently took the old woman's arm and led her down the hall. "The gentleman sitting across from you is a charming old fellow, don't you think?"

"I have no idea. I just met him and I don't even know his name. But I think he's as crazy as a hoot owl, calling me Kathy and kissing my hand."

The nurse's aide guided the elderly woman in a room adjacent from her own room. "Mr. Parker just arrived today." she said. "He's been terribly depressed, ever since his wife left him. His children think the only thing that may help him snap out of his depression is if he had some female company." The nurse's aide turned around and smiled at Marybeth. "And since you seemed to be so lonely, and sometimes very sad, I thought you might enjoy cheering Mr.

Parker up. Look, here is a picture of his wife. Marybeth held the frame close to her face. *A nice looking lady*, she thought.

"Well what do you want me to do?" Marybeth asked. "Pretend that I'm Kathy?"

"Well no," said the nurse's aide. "You shouldn't go that far, but it sure wouldn't hurt to be friendly. Maybe Mr. Parker will snap out of his depression, and then see you for who you are."

"Well, of course I'll be friendly – but don't expect anything more than that." Marybeth huffed. She returned to the table, and paused before sitting down. There was something familiar with Mr. Parker's bushy eyebrows. Bushy eyebrows she thought and smiled as she sat down. Her husband, what was his name again? No matter, he had bushy eyebrows. They were so bushy that she even tried to braid them once, and actually was successful with two tiny braids on each side. She began to giggle at the thought.

Mr. Parker took Marybeth's hand again. "You look so lovely tonight my dear." He said, "Especially when you are smiling."

A sudden warm rush caused Marybeth's cheeks to color in a rosy flush. She reached out and touched Mr. Parker's eyebrows. "They feel the same," she said and quickly pulled her hand back.

Marybeth tilted her head to the side. "Shall I show you the garden?"

"Yes, that would be wonderful." Mr. Parker stood up as tall as his stooped frame allowed, and offered his arm.

"Thank you," she whispered.

***

"Well that went better than I ever expected it to," Anita said to the other nurses' aides, as they stood in a half circle watching the old couple, walk through the portals and into the garden.

"Do you think Kathy will ever realize that Mr. Parker is her husband?" They asked each other.

"I don't think it really matters." Anita replied. "She may fall in love all over again. And I don't think Mr. Parker cares if she calls herself Marybeth, her twin sister's name, or her own name – *Kathy*. It's only a name." The young aides agreed, as they returned to their work with lightness in their step and a victory smile on their lips.

Suggestions for Discussions:

Who was your biggest love in your life? What was so special about that person?

Can you remember a particular nurse or nurse's aide that you thought was especially nice?

Or maybe you remember a certain priest, rabbi or nun that you were fond of?

Have you ever done any voluntary or charity work?

What did you do, and how did you feel about it?

ELEVEN

Cookie Fair

It was a day and a year ago,

My car got stuck under a rainbow,

In the middle of a field,

It wouldn't yield;

I needed a truck to tow.

I trudged to the next house by a lake.

The farmer smiled and gave me a handshake.

I cried, " My motor is down!

Need to get to town,

Or I'll never make it to the cookie bake!"

"Oh, you bake cookies for the fair?

Why I like cookies better than éclairs!

Git in my car,

It ain't so far,

Then we'll haul you back over there."

Well, I was pleased as Hawaiian punch.

Yup, you're right about that hunch.

The farmer and me

Kissed and got married,

And eat cookies under rainbows for lunch.

TWELVE

The 7 Sex Steps

author unknown

Only for readers older than 70 ☺

The 1st kind of sex is called – Smurf Sex.

This kind of sex happens when you first meet

someone, and you both have sex until you are blue in the face.

The 2nd kind of sex is called – Kitchen Sex. This is when you have been with your partner for a short time and you are so horny you will have sex anywhere, even in the kitchen.

The 3rd kind of sex is called – Bedroom Sex. This is when you have been with your partner for a long time. Your sex has gotten routine and you usually have sex only in your bedroom.

The 4th kind of sex is called - Hallway Sex. This is when you have been with your partner for too long. When you pass each other in the hallway and you both say "screw you."

The 5th kind of sex is called – Religious Sex. Which means you get Nun in the morning, Nun in the Afternoon and Nun at night. (very popular)

The 6th kind of sex is called – Courtroom Sex. This is when you cannot stand your wife any more. She takes you to court and screws you in front of everyone.

And last, but not least;

The 7th kind of sex is called – Social Security Sex.. You get a little each month, but not enough to live on.

THIRTEEN

Caramel Candy

Have you ever had a caramel stick to your

gums?

Can't get it down with the strength of your

tongue?

You suck it, you pick it, and you can't make

it fall,

You switch on the lamplight; in the mirror

you ball!

The bridges get loose; your fillings come

out,

You swear this ain't funny as you jump all

about.

No string is in sight to floss your teeth,

Aha! There's a garland lying right by the

wreath!

You step back from the window, don't

want anyone to see.

As you stuff garland ends so carefully,

Into your mouth to catch that mean old

caramel;

The tinsel tickles, your mouth starts to

swell.

***

Ding dong! Oh no who could that be?

With a sparkly mouth, you open the door

carefully.

Forgetting the caramel, you give your

friends a big hello

Your smile is full of glitter; you put on quite a show.

So now we have the start of a new fashion hit.
It's the sparkly teeth powder in the plastic kit!

A tinsel or two hanging down from your ears,
Makes a bombastic smile!
Cheers! And happy New Year!

FOURTEEN

A Calling

(A true story)

Have you ever experienced a calling? Yes we often hear this in a religious sense. When I was little, our neighbor's son chose to become a Catholic priest. In my childish wonderment, I asked him why. And his reply was simple; he had a *calling*.

Okay, I thought. *Someone gave him a call on his phone.* — But we all know *that* wasn't it.

A calling? Have you ever experienced such a feeling? I suppose it's when one is attracted to some endeavor, some mission, something inside of us that we can't even put to words. Do I have a calling? I think so – my calling is writing. Even as a child, I kept a journal. I collected pen pals, and I loved writing assignments in school. Yes, I guess you could say; that's a calling.

My son, Mike, had a calling too. Ever since he was knee high he was fascinated with fire engines. We bought him a book full of large glossy photos of fire engines. He couldn't stop leafing through it, and when he wasn't doing that, he was pushing his little fire truck, accompanied by siren sounds, that he blasted out, through his little cupid mouth, in perfect key.

At that time, we lived in a town house. My neighbor always knew when our Mike was sick; because that was the only time she didn't hear the fire truck sirens scream through our house walls, causing sound waves in her morning coffee.

This fascination with fire engines never ceased. Where we live, fire stations thrive on the local volunteers who live in the small towns and villages. Mike was a junior volunteer, and his work there, turned out to be his favorite hobby – right up to this day.

I remember one particular day, Mike was fifteen years old, and like a real fire man, he was allowed to bring his fireman suit and boots home. He lined them up near our front door, so that he could just leap into the boots, pull on the jacket and helmet, and rush to the fire station on his bicycle.

In case of fire or accidents, a siren blasted throughout our village, which I guarantee woke every man woman and child out of their deepest sleep.

Well, the first week had passed, without any incident. Mike always checked his firemen clothes, to make sure they were lined up just right. His bike was leaned against our house wall, in the direction of the fire house, and his helmet lay by his bed. I sometimes caught myself wishing for some harmless fire, just to satisfy my son's Good Samaritan needs.

And then it happened! One night, around 2:00 AM, the siren let out its ear splitting howl. It didn't take a minute till I heard our son, run down our corridor, leap into his fireman's attire, and slam the front door behind him. His Papa and I rushed to the kitchen window and watched our son, under the yellow street lights, push into those bicycle pedals like a mad man.

Funny thing though, the siren didn't stop. Papa and I remained at the window, to see if we could see any signs of smoke or flames, but the night was as clear as glass.

Suddenly my Hubby looked at me, lifted a finger, and said; "Listen! That's not a siren!"

He's right, I thought. The sound was too irregular, sometimes stopping, and then starting and stopping again.

"Oh my God!" We both exclaimed, and rushed to my son's bedroom window on the opposite side of the house.

There, we could see, sitting on our neighbors back steps, their huge German Shepard, crying like a baby for his owners to let him back in. His howls sounded exactly like the fire alarm sirens! After we finally caught our breath from laughing, snorting and knee slapping – the front door slowly opened.

Our puzzled and truly disappointed son gave us a sheepish grin. "Nobody was at the fire station", he mumbled. "I don't get it… the siren is still on."

We both felt so sorry for him. We weren't sure how to break the news.

But we didn't have to. – He heard it himself, and burst into hearty laughter. That night, the three of us got out the chocolate cake and milk from the fridge and allowed ourselves an early morning snack.

 I guess not only
people have callings…
some animals do too.

FIFTEEN

MOONLIGHT SEEKERS ON A
THREE-QUARTER NIGHT

We were a slinking and a crawlin',
Behind Gus's old chicken shed.
Ready to fetch us fresh eggs,
To go with our last crusty bread.

Maw-maw was out cleanin',

And Paw? Who the hell knows.

Nobody feeds us grub,

Nobody hears our woes.

Proud of our name:

"The Moonlight Seekers",

We tiptoed out, on our torn worn sneakers.

Not much more than 3 crates high,

We was: Beppo, Pete, Wally, 'n scarred up

Skye.

The moon gave off a perfect three quarter

light.

Better than a torch that glares way too

bright.

The chickens were squakin' as we ran up the
ramp.

A cry from the house;

"A tramp! A tramp!"

We grabbed the eggs, as carefully as we
could.

Didn't want them scrambled or fall on the
wood.

Skye tucked a big fat hen in his woven corn
sack.

Then we tumbled like pebbles out that
chicken shack.

When gun shots blasted round our ears!

I think Beppo peed, and Wally blubbered
tears!

'n standin' before us was Paw in his Sunday
shorts.

Behind him sweet flushed Miss Rose, who
was all out of sorts.

Paw got all red,
we could see in the light.
And Miss Rose was a wailin';
sort of a funny sight.

Then Paw grabbed us by the ears, and
hauled us inside.
Told us we didn't see nothing, or he'd tan
our hide!
Miss Rose chopped the chicken, then
scrambled the eggs,
While we all sat at the table and stared at
her legs.
We stuffed our empty bellies, then went
home to bed.
Yup we're the Moonlight Seekers;
Shhhh -Now enough is said.

SIXTEEN

OUR THOUGHTS ARE FREE

I do believe choosing and thinking our own thoughts is the greatest gift that we have.

For our thoughts are truly *ours*. And because they are our possession, we can *choose* to keep them to ourselves – or not.

No matter how our body changes in age, the memories we have stored, remain young and energetic. If we acknowledge them as a separate entity of our being, then we recognize that these memories haven't aged and never will. Isn't that just wonderful? Memories are truly our fountain of youth.

Of course it's hard when we experience physical pain. That can occupy us so intensely that there is no more room for any other thoughts. But if this pain is taken care of, through medication, through meditation and has hopefully lessened – then we are free to discover the power within us. We are able to turn our thoughts to the time when we were young, vital and excited about life and what it holds in store for us.

I have detached myself from what made me sad. Hah! Easier said than done, you probably say. You're right. And I'm not always successful either. But when I manage to set my thoughts back to better times, and feel the joy once again, it is worth the effort.

How do I do this? *I will share with you my secret.*

It's not about *just* letting go of the pain, the people, the grieving, or the circumstances that pull you down. It's about *replacing* those sad thoughts with new thoughts and feelings. It's about remembering the time when we were young, and happy. Maybe we were in love, maybe we accomplished a challenging task, or maybe we were with merry friends. Whatever that memory was ... it is stored in our brains, and has never disappeared. The memories are there for us to recall and hold in our thoughts at whim. **For what other reason, should we even keep these memories?**

How did we feel when we were young? We were gay, living in the moment, and saw the lighter side of life with humor and a youthful nonchalance. Or maybe the joyous feelings came later on in life: The new job, the first sale, holding a baby, taking a ride in a newly purchased car. Whatever it was; recall that moment. *You can do it.* And now, when the moment of joy has entered your mind, see it, and feel it before your mental eye, allowing it to fill your thoughts once more.

I can remember after something wonderful has happened to me, like a kiss, or a successful business day – how I would smile to myself at the thought, sometimes many days later. Why can't we still smile at the thought many *years* later? Who says we can't? *We can!* We can feel the thrill, the happiness, and the joy spreading within us again. Just set yourself back to that time.

It's truly liberating to steer our thoughts to places that make us feel better. And the magic is – when we do – happiness automatically enters our lives. People are more attracted to us. They don't see our age; they see our warm sincere smile, a smile that is inviting and far away from critique and scorn.

And our minds become alert, our hearts feel stronger, and we stand a bit straighter.

It's within every one of us. We just have to remember and dwell on that feeling till the good memories lighten out thoughts. It doesn't matter if it's only a memory. Memories are made for you to recall and enjoy again and again in your senior years.

Suggestions for Discussions:

When you think back, can you recall a happy moment that you'll never forget?

Family. Christmas, a new pet? Your wedding, the birth of your children.

a new home,

a raise,

a special vacation

joyous moments with friends?

SEVENTEEN

ABOUT THE AUTHOR

After raising two sons and retiring from the real-estate business, the author and her husband can be found traveling around the European continent in their caravan. Known as the 'story telling lady', many a story was born and typed on her trusty laptop while on the road. After writing and directing several plays and comedy skits, Angelika Schwarz is now focusing on writing novels and short stories.

If you enjoyed **Brighten a Senior's Day,**

then you'll be delighted with

Brighten a Senior's Day

II and III.

And if you like **romance/suspense**

Then

WINGS ON HER HEELS,

Will captivate you!

The novel can be purchased worldwide in

Amazon.

More about the Author, **Angelika Schwarz,**

and her upcoming books can be found online.

https://authorschwarz.wordpress.com

https://www.facebook.com/AuthorSchw

arz

https://twitter.com/AngelikaAuthor

Just a few of the reviews on

WINGS ON HER HEELS

"By far the best book I've read in ages."

"Superb Book!"

"Should be on the Best Seller list!

"…totally entertaining, fast moving novel, spiked with humour, and deep emotions. It's definitely a page turner!"

"I loved this book!!… Not a dull moment. It carried me from – cosy, touching, tender, moments to - sitting on the edge of my seat - moments. I'm definitely going to read it again. And I truly hope to see more of Angelika Schwarz's works."

"The writing of some of the events draws you right in - you can find yourself out of breath! The author knows how to write about emotions and longing for home. Looking forward to reading more from Angelika!!"

"Angelika Schwarz not only draws her readers immediately into her tale, she paints breath-taking landscapes with her words as well."

"...very exciting and a must read!!!"

"...From the first page on, I couldn't put WINGS ON HER HEELS down. It's about a small town girl following her inner longings. Beautiful, as well as, frightening scenes result in a cascade of realistic and sometimes breathless events."

"...The plot development had unexpected twists. Her imagery makes the reader feel like they are right there in Germany with Melanie."

"Good Show . . . Hungry for More"

"...the author kept suspense building. The book kept me reading until late into the night."

"Great book, with a twist, and characters you love to love and hate! Wonderful first novel, hope there's more to follow."

"...suspenseful and engaging. Wonderful book from a first time author, can't wait for more."

"Pour a glass of wine and cuddle up with a fantastic book...Great story, very hard to put down!"

Made in the USA
Monee, IL
26 February 2021